NEW ZEALAND
NATIONAL
PARKS

Lansdowne Press

WELDON·HARDIE
GROUP OF COMPANIES

RAY JOYCE

Acknowledgements
The publishers wish to thank the Department of
Conservation, the National Parks Centennial
Commission and Dr Gerry McSweeney for their
assistance in compiling this booklet.

Text and Design
Piers Hayman

Typeset in New Zealand by Saba Graphics Ltd,
Christchurch
Printed in Hong Kong through Colorcraft Ltd.

Published by Lansdowne Press, Auckland
a division of Rigby International
59 View Road, Glenfield
Auckland, New Zealand
© Copyright Lansdowne Press 1987.

ISBN 0–86866–108–2

CONTENTS

INTRODUCTION

For so young a species, *Homo sapiens* has had a profound effect on the planet Earth.

More than 600 million years ago, the first glimmerings of life appeared in the warm seas of the Pre-Cambrian period, but another 599 million years would pass before ape-like creatures began to experiment with primitive stone tools. Only within the last 10,000 years has man learned to cultivate plants and domesticate animals so, geologically speaking, our human era began only yesterday.

In this short space of time we have wrought such havoc with our exploding populations and our desperate search for food, fuel and raw materials, that we are already in danger of destroying the world we profess to own.

Only very recently have governments of human beings recognised the need to protect areas of the earth from the ravages of their own species. The first 'national park' was founded in Yellowstone, USA, and 15 years later, in 1887, the Ngati Tuwharetoa Maori people gifted 6500 acres of land around Tongariro to become the world's fourth national park, here in New Zealand. Since that time, national parks have been established in over 100 countries throughout the world, with New Zealand today being fortunate enough to have 15 to its credit.

New Zealand is unique in its geological history. This island group broke away from the prehistoric southern continent of Gondwanaland well before the evolution of the first mammals. Left in splendid isolation, it became a paradise for birds, for the only land mammals to reach these shores across the formidable barrier of open ocean were two species of bat. Fortunately, the finest remnants of this remarkable heritage have been preserved within the network of our national parks and reserves, for the devastation brought about by the arrival of man is not yet wholly complete. Compared to other countries, New Zealand was discovered and inhabited only recently, and although we have since managed to exterminate many of our native bird species, there are still enough survivors clinging to the last remains of their natural environment to make New Zealand national parks among the most fascinating in the world.

Controlled and administered by the Department of Conservation, the 15 parks offer the visitor a wide range of cultural features and recreational pursuits in a rich landscape of unparalleled variety. You may choose to walk through giant primeval forests, sail the blue waters of the Pacific, explore glaciers and active volcanic peaks, ski the mountain slopes, raft the rapids, paddle quietly along deserted waterways,

MAL CLARBROUGH/NELSON LAKES NATIONAL PARK

or simply pass the time in whatever way you please among the native plants and creatures for whom this country is home. Their ancestors have lived here since long before human beings were chipping their first stones — let alone building canoes or ships that would bring them across the seas to Aotearoa, the land of the long white cloud.

Our national parks are a precious part of our heritage. They are a treasure to be held in trust for the future, not only of our own species, but of those that were here before us.

Piers Hayman
1987

Left: Mitre Peak from Milford Sound, Fiordland National Park. *Above*: Mount Robert, Nelson Lakes National Park. *Right*: Native bush, Hauraki Gulf Maritime Park.

RAY JOYCE

5

BAY OF ISLANDS MARITIME AND HISTORIC PARK

Situated in the warm winterless north of New Zealand, the Bay of Islands Maritime and Historic Park stretches from Ranfurly Bay in the north, right down to the entrance of Whangaruru Harbour. In between lies the Bay of Islands itself, with more than 800 kilometres of indented coastline and countless islands, where the clear blue-green waters of the Pacific lap onto soft sandy beaches backed by the cool shade of ancient pohutukawa trees.

With its multitude of quiet coves and estuaries, and its broad stretches of sheltered water, the park is a sailors' paradise, but there are plenty of peaceful and secluded harbours or open sea beaches accessible to the land-bound visitor as well. Add to this magnificent views, numerous inland reserves and an area steeped in history, and you have an unmatched recipe for relaxation and recreation.

Notable attractions are boat trips among the islands, deep sea angling in the offshore coastal waters, or a visit to Waitangi, where the controversial treaty was signed in 1840 by Lieutenant-Governor Hobson and a group of Maori chiefs.

Above: Looking east to Cape Brett. *Above right*: Maori war canoe at Waitangi celebrations. *Below right*: Manuka in flower at Whangaruru. *Far right*: Low tide at Whangaroa Harbour.

RAY JOYCE

HAURAKI GULF MARITIME PARK

More than one fifth of New Zealand's total population lives in Auckland, making it hardly the sort of area one would associate with a national park. However, the 47 islands and 13,600 square kilometres that make up the Hauraki Gulf Maritime Park have been described as some of the finest sailing waters to be found anywhere in the world.

The islands provide almost limitless opportunities for picnics, barbecues, camping and walking, and at the same time shelter the gulf from the strong broad swells of the Pacific Ocean. Within this protective chain lies a huge maritime playground in which the mild and temperate climate provides ideal conditions for watersports of every description. These enviable facilities are enjoyed to the full by Aucklanders and visitors alike, and the host of craft that flock out onto the gulf on every available weekend have earned Auckland the title of 'City of Sails'.

Of special interest to the wildlife enthusiast are the seabirds, particularly the large numbers of petrels and shearwaters that come from distant oceans around the world to nest on the islands of the gulf. Some of these islands are set aside as reserves, and one of them, Little Barrier, has been a sanctuary since 1895 and is now home to many of New Zealand's unique and endangered birds.

C.R. VEITCH

Left: Looking east across the Hauraki Gulf from Wenderholm. *Above right:* The rare North Island saddleback has been recently reintroduced on Tiritiri Matangi Island, a nature reserve that is open to the public. *Below right:* Windsurfing off Takapuna beach.

RAY JOYCE

ANNEKE HAYMAN

10

UREWERA NATIONAL PARK

In the green wilderness of Urewera, time has stood still. The rugged country with its thick mantle of native bush has remained much the same for millions of years, and here it is possible to step from your car and walk back into the mists of prehistory.

The park contains the North Island's largest stretch of untouched native forest, in which you can tramp for days without ever meeting another human being. Even a short stroll down one of the park's more accessible and well maintained tracks will take you deep into a rich and luxuriant wonderland that has altered little since the time of the dinosaurs.

Until the coming of man, no mammals except bats reached New Zealand, which is one of the reasons why our native forests and the widlife they contain are so precious and so unique. The Urewera National Park offers excellent opportunities to observe forest birds in their natural surroundings and, to add to this, the rare blue duck is still to be found among the rapids and dramatic waterfalls of the Aniwaniwa Stream. Lake Waikaremoana, into which this stream flows, is renowned as one of New Zealand's most beautiful lakes, and some of the finest views of bush and lake scenery can be obtained simply by driving along State Highway 38, which runs through the centre of the park.

ANNEKE HAYMAN

ANNEKE HAYMAN

Left: Mist in the Urewera forest. *Above right*: Bridal Veil falls on the Aniwaniwa Stream. *Below right*: Sunlight dapples a moss-covered tree trunk by a forest track.

CRAIG POTTON

TONGARIRO NATIONAL PARK

New Zealand's first national park, and only the fourth in the world, Tongariro is the best known and most visited of all our parks. The main routes down the North Island pass by it, and the dramatic peaks of its three spectacular volcanoes dominate the surrounding countryside. Ngauruhoe, Ruapehu and Mount Tongariro itself are all still very much alive, and the rumblings and smokings of their changing moods are a constant reminder of the immense forces of nature that created this landscape.

Opportunities for tramping abound, with a network of tracks and overnight huts providing everything from a short stroll to a protracted hike in a surprising variety of different surroundings. Bush, river, mountain, lake, thermal spring and desert wilderness are all features of the Tongariro National Park, and in the winter the skifields of Mount Ruapehu provide excitement and enjoyment for thousands of winter sport enthusiasts.

Above: Ngauruhoe from across the desert wilderness. *Right*: Crater Lake, Mount Ruapehu.

JOHN OMBLER/D.O.C.

WHANGANUI NATIONAL PARK

One of the youngest of our national parks, Whanganui was officially opened in February 1987. On either side of the long, winding ribbon of the Wanganui River, the 79,000 hectares that make up the park include high cliffs, areas of lowland forest and many Maori historical sites.

Exploration by jet-boat, raft or canoe affords many visitors the exhilarating challenge of turbulent rapids, or the quiet tranquillity of long, peaceful gorges. For those who come on foot, there are several walkways and tracks on which they can lose themselves for days, while others simply enjoy the history and scenic beauty of the river through the many features that are accessible by road. With its central location and river access, Whanganui National Park is one of the most easily available wilderness experiences.

Left: A majestic northern rata stands above the Wanganui River near Otaihanga.

EGMONT NATIONAL PARK

Towering 2518 metres above the Taranaki country-side, the solitary cone of Taranaki/Mount Egmont displays the classical symmetry that is characteristic of andesitic volcanoes throughout the world. Dormant since the mid-1700s, the mountain has become a land-based island, a unique world in which the regenerating vegetation and its accompanying wildlife have been dominated and controlled by isolation, height and climate. The park itself is almost a complete circle with a radius of 9.6 kilometres and the mountain peak at the centre. Only to the north west is the symmetry broken, by a bulge towards a small offshoot that encompasses the Kaitake Range.

Almost 300 kilometres of walking and tramping tracks criss-cross the lower slopes, and even a drive up one of the sealed access roads provides a vivid demonstration of the effects of altitude on the mountain flora. The higher one goes, the smaller the trees become. Soon they are little more than shrubs, then low bushes, and finally only tussocks and herbs. For the hardier visitor, a climb reveals that higher still the tussocks give way to lichens and mosses, and then there is nothing but the bare rock of ancient lava flows radiating down from the summit.

The mountain climate can be harsh and temperamental, and on the upper levels there is no shelter from winds or bad weather that can arrive very rapidly indeed. For this reason, visitors to the park are urged to treat Taranaki/Mount Egmont with the respect that it deserves.

RAY JOYCE

RAY JOYCE

Above right: The white-topped cone of Taranaki/Mount Egmont seen from Cape Egmont. *Below right*: Snow dusts the summit of the mountain.

MARLBOROUGH SOUNDS MARITIME PARK

The drowned river valleys and numerous wooded islands of the Marlborough Sounds contain some of the most popular summer resort areas in New Zealand. The intricate maze of sheltered waterways and secluded inlets offers unmatched opportunities for cruising and exploration by boat, and there are enough roads and tracks to afford ample access for the land-bound visitor.

The Marlborough Sounds Maritime Park includes more than 100 separate reserves, and there are walking and tramping tracks that provide anything from a 15-minute stroll to a three-day hike. Campsites abound, and free camping is permitted over large areas in most of the reserves. Some of the most beautiful and tranquil corners of the Sounds are accessible only by boat, which is one of the extra attractions of a maritime park. For visitors who arrive by road, it is possible to arrange for boat transport to any destination within the park.

Spectacular views, mountain scenery, sparkling sea, and above all peace and tranquillity: these are the hallmarks of the Marlborough Sounds.

Above: Looking east over the Marlborough Sounds with Croiselles Harbour on the left. *Above right*: Many parts of the park can best be explored by boat. *Below right*: Rat-free island reserves are refuges for some of New Zealand's unique wildlife, such as the Tuatara, the only survivor of an ancient order of reptiles.

16

ABEL TASMAN NATIONAL PARK

Abel Tasman National Park, with an area of 18,000 hectares, is the smallest national park in the country. It is also rather remote from the mainstream of New Zealand's tourist trail, but if you are a lover of unspoilt golden beaches, clear blue sea, and rich green forest that tumbles to the tideline, then Abel Tasman is the place for you.

The main attraction for most of the park's visitors is access to an unbelievable chain of idyllic beaches. There are plenty of camping sites and walking tracks, and each bay is more beautiful than the last. Even though the area has been extensively modified by European settlement, it is still fascinating to explore the inland tracks for traces of the region's history, or delve into the mysteries of Harwood's Hole and its associated cave systems.

Abel Tasman is a perfect blend of forest, beach and sea. Successful control of fire by park staff has made it an exciting experiment in the regeneration of native bush.

Right: The headquarters of the Abel Tasman National Park are located close to this magnificent beach at Totaranui.

NELSON LAKES NATIONAL PARK

Some 16,000 years ago, the northern part of the South Island gradually emerged from the last cold grip of the ice age. As the ice retreated, it left behind two immense scars that had been carved out of solid rock by the grinding force of massive glaciers. Now filled with water, these scars have become Lakes Rotoiti and Rotoroa, the two lakes which, with their watersheds, form the Nelson Lakes National Park.

The area is a wilderness of mountain, lake and beech forest; trampers, mountaineers, geologists and naturalists are all attracted to its wild and rugged beauty. On the lakes themselves, opportunities for water sport bring canoeists and sailors to the park, while anglers can try their skills on lake and stream.

New Zealand native plants have evolved no protection against browsing mammals, so introduced deer and chamois have played havoc with the balance of the country's ecology. Hunting permits are available in Nelson Lakes and other national parks as a measure to control these unwanted species that have no natural predators to limit their numbers.

Good road access, magnificent scenery and a host of recreational opportunities make Nelson Lakes well worth the visit.

Above: Mount Robert mirrored in the still waters of Lake Rotoiti. *Right*: The Cupola basin and Mount Hopeless.

ARTHUR'S PASS NATIONAL PARK

Arthur's Pass cuts through the jagged backbone of the South Island, and is one of only five road routes that connects the east coast with the west. The park's alpine passes were initially used by the Maori to reach the West Coast greenstone. Arthur's Pass provided the first road access from Canterbury to the goldfields, and later the railway followed the same route.

The 100,000 hectares of the national park offer the most varied and readily accessible opportunities for mountain recreation anywhere in New Zealand. It is a region of rugged peaks, steep, bush-covered valleys, sheer cliffs, high waterfalls, and racing torrents that boil and tumble through deep gorges before flooding out onto the wide, shingle river-beds that are so characteristic of the South Island.

The range of activities available within the park includes tramping, skiing, climbing and nature walks, with adventure camps and park interpretation programmes periodically arranged for younger visitors. Notable amongst the park's wildlife is the kea, the New Zealand mountain parrot. Owing to a belief that keas attacked sheep, these unfortunate birds suffered a long period of persecution, but now they are fully protected. Perhaps it is justifiable retaliation that prompts the kea's mischievous persecution of visitors!

P. SIMPSON/ARTHUR'S PASS NATIONAL PARK

ANNEKE HAYMAN

Left: The Devils Punchbowl boasts a spectacular 140-metre waterfall. *Above right*: Mount Rolleston, one of the many peaks that dominate the skyline of the park. *Below right*: The kea is New Zealand's mountain parrot.

RAY JOYCE

RAY JOYCE

CRAIG POTTON

24

WESTLAND NATIONAL PARK

Fox and Franz Josef Glaciers are undoubtedly the best known and most dramatic of Westland's scenic attractions. They are two vast rivers of ice, each descending some 11 kilometres from the perpetual snows of the high mountain slopes down into the heart of a lush green rain forest, which lies only 250 metres above sea level. Here, on a hot summer's day, you can step from the shade of the bush and a few moments later be standing on the cold blue ice of a glacier — an unforgettable and incomparable experience.

But there is more to Westland National Park than the two main glaciers. The mountains and snowfields of the Southern Alps' Great Divide form the park's eastern boundary, and between the mountain tops and the sea lie 60 more glaciers as well as alpine grasslands, waterfalls, rivers, lakes, forests and hot springs. In the short 30 kilometres from east to west the land drops from the 3498 metres of Mount Tasman right down to sea level, and the variety of scenery and plant and animal life within that small area is quite remarkable.

Westland National Park is a place of contrasts, leaving the visitor with a lasting impression of tall, snow-covered peaks glimpsed through a luxuriant curtain of rimu rain forest.

Above left: Visitors explore the ice-scraped rocks at Franz Josef. *Below left:* Lichen on Sentinel Rock, the first signs of regenerating vegetation after glacier retreat. *Left:* The park stretches from the Tasman Sea, eastwards to the mountains of the Great Divide. *Above:* The cold blue ice of the Franz Josef Glacier.

C.R. VEITCH

MOUNT COOK NATIONAL PARK

Within the 70,013 hectares of Mount Cook National Park lie most of New Zealand's highest mountains. More than one third of the park lies permanently under snow and ice, and the 21-kilometre-long Tasman Glacier is not only the largest glacier in the park, but also one of the largest in the world outside the polar regions.

Mount Cook itself towers above its neighbours, and at 3764 metres is New Zealand's tallest mountain, but in and around the park there are at least 30 peaks that clear 3000 metres, and another 150 over 2000 metres. This is real mountain country, rugged and unyielding, so it is surprising that the park can offer such a wide range of recreational activities. As well as climbing, skiing and scenic flights from Mount Cook's airfield, there are opportunities for tramping, walking, and white water rafting.

Cold clear days characterise the Mount Cook winter, but in spring and summer the sun is warm, and the alpine plants splash touches of colour among the jumbled rocks. South Island edelweiss, mountain daisy and snow tussock are among the better known, with the giant mountain buttercup, or 'Mount Cook lily', being the most famous of all.

RAY JOYCE

Above left: The diminutive rock wren lives among the scrub and boulders of the Southern Alps. *Below left*: The Mount Cook lily is not really a lily at all, but a form of mountain buttercup. *Right*: The towering summit of Mount Cook, New Zealand's tallest mountain.

26

ANNEKE HAYMAN

ANNEKE HAYMAN

MOUNT ASPIRING NATIONAL PARK

Named after the massive 3035-metre wedge of Mount Aspiring, the park comprises 287,163 hectares of untamed alpine wilderness stretching westwards from the heads of Lake Wakatipu and Wanaka almost to the Tasman Sea. The western side, in particular, is as remote and far away from roads as anywhere in New Zealand. Access throughout the park is difficult, but in the east a range of tracks and huts offer the hardy tramper lush and colourful valleys surrounded by magnificent mountain scenery. The transalpine Routeburn Track is one of the best known. Some of the finest climbing in the country is provided by the mountains themselves, but all visitors should bear in mind that, in this type of country, the weather can change very quickly indeed, and storms can be dangerous for the unprepared.

A more leisurely way to appreciate the savage beauty of Mount Aspiring National Park is by driving up one of the lake-head roads or, better still, by following State Highway 6 as it crosses the famous Haast Pass at the northern end of the park. The pass offers a breathtaking succession of views of forests, hills, mountains and lakes.

Far left: The upper reaches of the Haast River. *Left*: Flowering southern rata splashes red among the green on the forested walls of Haast Pass. *Above*: Storm clouds blowing away from the summit of Mount Aspiring.

29

FIORDLAND NATIONAL PARK

Fiordland is one of the largest National Parks in the world. It contains 1.2 million hectares of dense forests, snow-capped mountains, deep glacial valleys, crystal lakes and steep-sided fiords whose sheer walls drop 1500 metres to the water and carry straight on down for hundreds of fathoms more. The park boasts one of the world's highest waterfalls, and extensive areas of beech forest. It is the last home of one of New Zealand's rarest birds, the Takahe. Its famous Milford Track has been described as the finest walk in the world, and if you need further superlatives, Fiordland also has New Zealand's heaviest rainfall, deepest lake (Hauroko), and arguably its densest and most active population of sandflies.

Lakes Manapouri and Te Anau are gateways to the park. Visitors travel along the 120-kilometre road from Te Anau to Milford, a route that climbs through a mountain wonderland to the forbidding face of the Homer Saddle. Here a 1200-metre tunnel cuts through a wall of solid rock to take the road on down the Cleddau Valley to Milford. A launch trip is the best way to appreciate the special beauty of Milford Sound, whose southern wall is dominated by the 1692-metre Mitre Peak. Further south, the equally spectacular Doubtful Sound can be reached by launch across Lake Manapouri to a road connection over Wilmot Pass.

The more active visitor may explore the wild and rugged landscape of the park from one of the many walking or tramping tracks, the ultimate way to truly experience the grandeur and solitude that is Fiordland.

Right. The settlement of Milford is dwarfed by the surrounding mountains.

RAY JOYCE

PAPAROA NATIONAL PARK

Although only 28,000 hectares in area, Paparoa National Park, approved in principle in 1986, stretches from the coastal grandeur of the Punakaiki 'pancake rocks', back through the forests and river gorges of the western lowlands to the tussock tops and craggy peaks of the Paparoa Range. Landscape sculptured from limestone dominates, with deep gorges and intricate networks of caves and sink holes. Nikau palm forest gives the coastline a subtropical appearance, while inland the lowland forest has the highest recorded densities of bird life in New Zealand.

There is a wide variety of short, easy walks, along the coast and up the gorges, leading inland to more adventurous tramping tracks that are fascinating for both naturalist and historian alike. An old pack track from the gold rush days traverses the park, and yet the highlands and hidden valleys beyond have remained largely free from the ravages of mining, farming or logging. Here is a complete natural paradise unrivalled in its rich complexity — a worthy new addition to the list of New Zealand national parks.

Left: The picturesque gorge of the Fox River.